FESTIVE FOODS

JAPAN

Sylvia Goulding

CHELSEA
CLUBHOUSE
An Imprint of Chelsea House Publishers

Chelsea Clubhouse
An imprint of Chelsea House Publishers
132 West 31st Street
New York, NY 10001

Library of Congress Cataloging-in-Publication Data

Goulding, Sylvia.
  Festive foods / Sylvia Goulding. – 1st ed.
    v. cm.
  Includes bibliographical references and index.
  Contents: [1] China – [2] France – [3] Germany – [4] India – [5] Italy – [6] Japan – [7] Mexico – [8] United States.
  ISBN 978-0-7910-9751-9 (v. 1) – ISBN 978-0-7910-9752-6 (v. 2) – ISBN 978-0-7910-9756-4 (v. 3) – ISBN 978-0-7910-9757-1 (v. 4) – ISBN 978-0-7910-9753-3 (v. 5) – ISBN 978-0-7910-9754-0 (v. 6) – ISBN 978-0-7910-9755-7 (v. 7) – ISBN 978-0-7910-9758-8 (v. 8)
  1. Cookery, International. 2. Gardening. 3. Manners and customs. I. Title.
  TX725.A1G56 2008
  641.59–dc22
                              2007042722

Chelsea Clubhouse books are available at special discounts when purchased in bulk quantities for businesses, associations, institutions, or sales promotions. Please call our Special Sales Department in New York at (212) 967-8800 or (800) 322-8755.

You can find Chelsea Clubhouse on the World Wide Web at **http://www.chelseahouse.com**

Printed and bound in Dubai

10 9 8 7 6 5 4 3 2 1

For The Brown Reference Group plc.:
Project Editor: Sylvia Goulding
Cooking Editor: Angelika Ilies
Contributors: Jacqueline Fortey, Sylvia Goulding
Photographers: Klaus Arras, Lucy Suleiman
Cartographer: Darren Awuah
Art Editor: Paula Keogh
Illustrator: Jo Gracie
Picture Researcher: Mike Goulding
Managing Editor: Bridget Giles
Production Director: Alastair Gourlay
Editorial Director: Lindsey Lowe
Children's Publisher: Anne O'Daly

Photographic Credits:
Front Cover: Shutterstock (inset); Klaus Arras (main)
Back Cover: Klaus Arras
Alamy: LMR Group 6, fStop 24; **iStock:** title page, 3, 41; **Paula Keogh:** 7, 9, 13, 36; **Shutterstock:** 1, 3, 4, 5, 7, 8, 10, 12, 16, 19, 20, 22, 23, 28, 30, 31, 35, 38, 39, 40.

With thanks to models:
Caspar, Mariam, Miho, and Nils

Cooking Editor
Angelika Ilies has always been interested in cookery and other countries. She studied nutritional sciences in college. She has lived in the United States, England, and Germany. She has also traveled extensively and collected international recipes on her journeys. Angelika has written more than 70 cookbooks and cooking card series. She currently lives in Frankfurt, Germany, with her two children and has spent much time researching children's nutrition. Both children regularly cook with their mother.

Contents

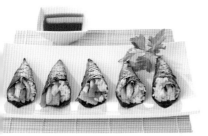

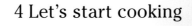

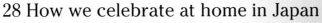

let's START COOKING

Cooking is fun—you learn about different ingredients and cooking methods, you find out how things taste, and you can serve a meal to your family and friends that you have cooked yourself! Some of the recipes in this book have steps that need adult help—ask a parent or other adult if they will be your kitchen assistant while you cook a meal.

This line tells you how many people the meal will feed.

In this box, you find out which ingredients you need for your meal.

WHAT YOU NEED:

SERVES 4 PEOPLE:

2¼ cups white rice
4 eggs, beaten
light soy sauce
4 tablespoons
    groundnut
    or soy oil
2 green onions
⅓ cup peeled shrimps
⅓ cup ham
⅓ cup green peas

Check before you start that you have everything at home. If something is missing, write it on your shopping list. Get all the ingredients ready before you start cooking.

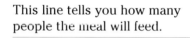

One of the great things about cooking is that you get to taste all the food first. That helps your cooking skills, too. You learn how to make it all taste better.

! WHEN TO GET help

Most cooking involves cutting ingredients and heating them in some way, whether frying, boiling, or cooking in the oven. Each time you see this exclamation mark, be extra careful as you cook and make sure your adult kitchen assistant is around to help.

For many meals you need to chop vegetables into small strips. Wash all the vegetables first. Trim off any parts that are starting to wilt or turn yellow. Cut off any stems, peel the vegetables, and scrape out seeds, if there are any. Cut the good parts of the vegetables into fine strips. Try and cut all the strips into similar lengths and shapes so they cook evenly.

Nori and other seaweeds are featured in many Japanese dishes. Boil the seaweed in a saucepan of water, and leave it to bubble for about 2 minutes. Lift the seaweed out of the pan. When it is cool enough to handle, cut it into the shape you need with scissors. You can also cut or crumble it into small pieces and add it to soups and other dishes as a garnish. Some seaweed is sold as flakes.

Chopsticks are tools that Japanese people use instead of knives and forks to eat their food. It is fun to try using them.

Japanese **table settings** are very stylish. People often use square plates. The plates might be black, white, or red.

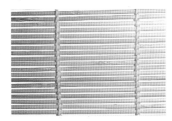

To make sushi, Japanese people use a **sushi rolling mat**. The mat is usually made from bamboo sticks.

A **tea whisk** is one of many tools people use for the Japanese tea ceremony. It is used to whisk up the tea paste.

A trip around
JAPAN

Japan is a fascinating country full of contrasts. It has modern hi-tech cities as well as traditional customs. Its food is among the best in the world.

Japan is an island state. It consists of four main islands and more than 4,000 smaller ones. The country lies in the Pacific Ocean. It is separated from the east coasts of China and Russia by the Sea of Japan. Japan's total land area is roughly that of California.

Japan has many mountains and active volcanoes. Its fast-flowing rivers have carried soil from the mountains to form fertile plains along the coast. These plains now make up most of Japan's farming land. The climate is similar to that of the East Coast.

Japan has about 127 million inhabitants. Most live in crowded cities along the coast. The capital is Tokyo. Other important cities are Yokohama, Osaka, Nagoya, Sapporo, and Kobe.

Ring of Fire

Japan lies in the Pacific Ring of Fire. This is an arc-shaped line around the Pacific Ocean where many volcanoes and earthquakes occur. Earth's crust is made of huge plates that meet in places such as the Pacific Ring of Fire.

These plates are moving, which can cause earthquakes and make volcanoes erupt. Japan has about 200 volcanoes and nearly one-third are active. People in Japan have to build houses and office buildings that can survive earthquakes. They also use early warning systems.

◁ *The official language* of Japan is Japanese. Many people also understand and speak some English. The main religions in Japan are Shinto and Buddhism.

Japan is in north-eastern Asia. It has four large and more than 4,000 small islands. Its nearest mainland neighbors are Russia, Korea, and China.

2

Japan's mountains, such as the Zao range, are often covered in snow and ideal for skiing. There are also crater lakes, more than 100 hot springs, and superb scenery.

ASIA

AFRICA

JAPAN

CHINA

RUSSIA

3

Kyushu Island is in the south of Japan. It has mild winters. At the south of the island, coral reefs attract divers. Inland, there are many hot springs, fertile valleys, and mountain ranges.

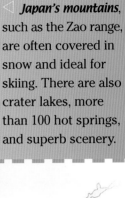

HOKKAIDO
● Sapporo

SEA OF JAPAN

(EAST SEA)

2

JAPAN

HONSHU

TOKYO

5

Kyoto ●
Kobe ● ● Nagoya

Hiroshima ● ● Osaka

1

SHIKOKU

Tokyo, Japan's capital city, has low-lying areas, high mountains, and even some volcanic islands within its city limits.

Nagasaki
●

KYUSHU

5

3

4

PACIFIC
OCEAN

This floating torii marks the entrance to a sacred site, the Shinto Itsukushima Shrine near Hiroshima.

4

The Ring of Fire is an area around the edges of the Pacific Ocean. Earthquakes and volcanic eruptions are a constant danger to cities nearby.

Hokkaido Island

Hokkaido is Japan's most northern and second largest island. Here the summers are warm and the winters are long and harsh. It has many mountains, with lakes and rivers, and some flatter areas on the coasts. Visitors come to ski in winter, or to visit its national parks and underground hot-water springs.

Honshu Island

Honshu is Japan's largest island, and so it is also called the mainland. Most people live here. More than twelve million people live in Tokyo, the bustling capital. With its suburbs and surroundings, the city is one of the most populated cities on Earth.

The Japanese Alps sweep down the center of Honshu Island. Mount Fuji (12,388 feet) is an extinct volcano near the capital. It is famous for its beautiful shape and snow-covered top, and is the country's national symbol. Three hundred miles west of Tokyo is Lake Biwa, Japan's largest freshwater lake.

▽ **Mount Fuji** is Japan's highest mountain and an extinct volcano, so it will no longer erupt. Its summit is often shrouded in clouds and mist, making it hard to see.

△ **Heian Jingu** in Kyoto is one of more than 90,000 Shinto shrines in Japan. Shinto is Japan's main religion. Many Shinto shrines look like Buddhist temples, and they are often colored red. Each temple has a gate, called a *torii*.

Shikoku Island

Shikoku is separated from Honshu by the Inland Sea, which is dotted with small islands. The islands are linked by several long bridges. Shikoku has mountains in the center and coral reefs on its southwestern coast. The climate is mild but rainy and stormy in summer.

Kyushu Island

Kyushu has broad plains and steep mountains. Mount Aso (5,223 feet), Japan's tallest active volcano, is here. On the western side, near the city of Nagasaki, lie the Unzen volcanoes. From time to time, deadly flows of hot gas and rock sweep down into the valleys. But the volcanoes also make spectacular scenery, fertile volcanic soil, and health-giving hot springs. Kyushu's cities and its farms are in the west.

Okinawa

Okinawa is a region. It includes three island groups and stretches for 600 miles southwest of Kyushu. Okinawa Island has superb beaches, caves, and small fishing villages. The seas around the southern islands contain coral reefs that teem with fish and other sealife.

SHAKY GROUND

On average, Japan has three minor earthquakes every day. The worst happened in 1923; 100,000 people died. An earthquake in Kobe in 1995 killed 6,000 people and destroyed 285,000 homes.

The food we grow in
JAPAN

Only a small part of the Japanese countryside can be farmed, but its coasts provide plenty of food.

Mountains and swamplands dominate large stretches of land, so cultivation is limited to the low-lying valleys and plains. Here water-loving plants, such as rice, thrive.

Northern farms

Hokkaido is Japan's most important island for growing food. It has large dairy farms that produce milk and cheese. Animals are reared for beef, pork, and mutton. Crops grown in the north include rice, potatoes, barley, beans, cabbages, beans, and onions, as well as apples and pears. Soba (buckwheat) from here is used to make the world-famous soba noodles.

Hokkaido is also known for its fish and seafood. Crab in particular is prized for its excellent flavor. Scallops, sea urchins, salmon, herring, flounder, cod, squid, octopus, shrimps, abalone, and kelp are also caught.

Mainland crops

On Honshu Island the landscape is rugged, so most crops are grown on the lower hillsides and flat ground. Rice is Japan's staple (most important) food. It is prepared in both sweet

THIRTY-A-DAY

Japanese people eat more than fish, soybeans, and rice. In fact, children are taught to eat 30 different foods a day, and 100 a week!

◁ *Green tea* is grown at the foot of Mount Fuji. Together with tea from Kyoto, it is considered among the best. Green tea is such a popular drink that people only speak of "tea" or "Japanese tea." Green tea is never drunk with milk or sugar.

and savory dishes. Rice farmers grow medium-grain rice in wet, muddy fields called paddies. After cooking, the rice grains stick together, which makes it ideal for sushi.

Honshu has vast plantations of green tea. Juicy oranges do well along the warm coast of the Inland Sea. The soybeans, or *edamame*, that grow here are made into many different soy sauces and into a beancurd called tofu.

Mainland livestock

Most beef cattle are farmed in the west of Honshu Island. The world-famous and expensive Kobe beef is made from black Wagyu cattle, which came originally from the port of Kobe. Farmers also keep dairy cows to supply milk to large cities. Pigs are raised all over Japan.

The South

The climate in Kyushu and Shikoku is mild, and the winters on the Pacific coast are warm. Farmers grow rice, sweet potatoes, cucumbers, eggplants, peppers, sugarcane, mandarin oranges, peaches, persimmons, grapes, lemons, bananas, and beans. Herds of beef cattle graze in Kyushu's pastures and farmers keep poultry for eggs and meat.

On Shikoku's eastern plains, cereals grow well. Some southern areas produce two crops of rice, wheat, and barley a year. Farmers also

▽ *Pigs are raised* all over Japan, and pork is a popular meat. It is eaten as cutlets, ground in dumplings, cold as pork shabu shabu, in stir-fries, in a sweet and sour sauce, or boiled.

grow vegetables and fruit under plastic here so they can be harvested early. But many people from Shikoku and other rural parts of Japan are leaving the countryside. They are moving to the cities in search of work.

Fishing

Japan has one of the world's largest fishing fleets. Its trawlers net large amounts of fish in the deep sea. Local fishermen catch fish from shallow waters along Japan's long coastlines. Hokkaido's waters produce catches of herring, cod, halibut, and squid. The catches have been smaller in recent years, so more fish are now imported from other countries. Freshwater fish farms raise trout and salmon, and seawater fish farms raise shrimps, sea bream, and seaweed.

Japan's most popular delicacies—sushi and sashimi—are made with raw fish. In the large fishing ports, such as Hachinhohe in northeastern Honshu, huge catches of fish can be frozen, stored, and processed so the fish gets to market fresh from the sea.

新さんま

Fish for sale at Tsukiji fish market in Tokyo. This fish market is one of the largest in the world. It handles more than 400 types of fish, shellfish, and seaweed. On sale are anything from tiny sardines to 660-pound tuna fish.

THE SECRET OF LONG LIFE

The people of Okinawa are known to reach old age—on average just over 90 years. Scientists think the secret of their success is an active life as fishermen and farmers and their healthy diet.

let's make...
SUPER SUSHI

Seafood is freely available along the Japanese coasts, rice flourishes in the fertile south of Japan, while nori seaweed grows mainly in the warm waters around Kyushu Island.

WHAT YOU NEED:

FOR THE SUSHI RICE:

1⅛ cups short- or medium-grain rice
1 small piece of dried nori seaweed
3 tablespoons rice vinegar
(or mild cider vinegar)
2 teaspoons sugar
½ teaspoon salt

FOR THE FILLING:

2 eggs
1 tablespoon soy sauce
1 teaspoon oil
¼ cucumber
1 carrot
¼ white daikon radish
a few curly endive lettuce or sorrel leaves
10 sheets dried roasted nori seaweed

2–3 teaspoons green Japanese horseradish paste (wasabi)

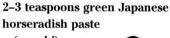

◁ To make this cone of sushi, you don't even need a sushi mat. You can just roll it in your hands.

1 Wash the rice and drain it in a sieve. Put it in a saucepan. Add ¾ pints water and the nori. Bring it to a boil over low heat. Boil for 2 minutes in bubbling water.

3 Meanwhile, heat the vinegar in a small saucepan. Add the sugar and salt and stir until both have dissolved. Put the rice into a wide bowl and stir in the vinegar mixture. Allow to cool until you can touch the rice. Place a damp cloth over the bowl.

4 Crack the eggs into a cup. Stir in 1 tablespoon soy sauce. Heat the oil in a nonstick skillet. Add the egg mixture and fry an omelet. Take it out, let it cool, then cut it into strips.

2 Fish out the nori. Turn the heat to very low and cover the saucepan. Simmer the rice for about 20 minutes. Stir from time to time. Turn off the heat and take off the lid. Cover the saucepan with a clean cloth, replace the lid, and allow to stand for 10 minutes.

5 Wash and trim the carrot and radish. Cut both into slices, then into thin strips. Cook the carrot strips for 2 minutes in boiling water so they are still crunchy. Drain. Wash lettuce or sorrel, pat dry, and tear into small pieces. Cut the nori sheets into fourths.

6 Hold a nori piece in your hand. Place on top 1 teaspoon sushi rice, cucumber strips, salad shreds, omelet and vegetable strips, and a little wasabi. Roll up the sheet to form a cone. Serve with soy sauce.

let's make...
FRIED TOFU

Tofu is a favorite meal of Buddhist monks, who eat no meat. Today it is a popular food all over Japan; especially in Kyoto, the town of 1,500 Buddhist temples.

WHAT YOU NEED:

SERVES 4 PEOPLE:

1 lb 2 ounces tofu
4 tablespoons flour
2 eggs
¾ cup sesame seeds
6 tablespoons oil

FOR THE SAUCE:

½ cup soy sauce
6 tablespoons rice vinegar
1 teaspoon ground pepper
a pinch of chili powder
2 teaspoons sugar

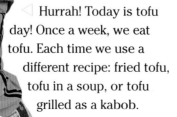

◁ Hurrah! Today is tofu day! Once a week, we eat tofu. Each time we use a different recipe: fried tofu, tofu in a soup, or tofu grilled as a kabob.

WHAT DOES <u>tofu</u> TASTE LIKE?

Tofu has little flavor of its own, but it picks up the flavor of the other ingredients in the same dish or of a sauce. Vegetarians often use tofu instead of meat.

1 Cut the tofu into ½-inch-thick slices. Cut the slices into strips, about 1 inch by 2 inches. **!**

2 Put the flour in a deep plate. Crack the eggs onto a second plate and beat them with a fork. Spread out the sesame seeds on a third plate.

3 Turn the tofu first in the flour, then in the egg, and finally in the sesame seeds, so it is covered in seeds all over, on both sides. In a small bowl, combine all the ingredients for the sauce.

4 Heat the oil in a wide skillet until it is hot but has not yet started smoking. Add the tofu strips and fry them for 2–3 minutes. Turn them with a wooden spoon and fry the other side for 2–3 minutes. Serve with the sauce.

USING *tofu*

Tofu goes well with other foods. You can even use it in Western recipes, for example to make burgers or in meat pies.

MY TIP

Tofu does not keep very well. Eat it on the day you buy it, or keep it in some cold water in the fridge and eat the next day.

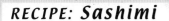

let's make...
SASHIMI

Sashimi means "raw seafood." Fish is perfectly safe to eat raw, if it is of good quality and very fresh. And Japan with its long coastlines has no shortage of fresh fish and seafood.

▽ I like all kinds of fish. My Mom says fish is brain food. Apparently it has lots of omega-3 oils in it and so it makes you intelligent too.

WHAT YOU NEED:

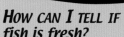

SERVES 4 PEOPLE:

1 small carrot
1 small piece of radish (about 2 inches)
1 small piece of cucumber (about 2 inches)
1 small unwaxed lemon
some cilantro leaves or flat-leaved parsley
1 lb very fresh salmon fillet (alternatively use a mixture of very fresh salmon fillet, very fresh tuna fillet, cooked and peeled giant shrimps, and fresh scallops)

4 roasted nori sheets
4 teaspoons wasabi paste
10 tablespoons soy sauce

HOW CAN I TELL IF <u>fish is fresh?</u>

<u>Whole fish should have:</u>
• moist, slippery skin • scales firmly attached to the body
• bright, moist gills • firm flesh
• clear eyes • a fresh smell
<u>Fish fillets or steaks should have:</u> • firm flesh • a clear and even color (white or red)
• a moist look • a fresh smell

1 Peel the carrot, cucumber, and radish. Trim the ends. Scrape out the cucumber seeds. Cut all into thin, finger-long strips. Scrub the lemon under hot water and pat it dry. Cut it with its zest into thin slices. Wash the cilantro and pat it dry.

2 Wash all the fish and seafood you are using under cold water. Pat dry with paper towels. Cut the fish across the fibers, into ½-inch-thick slices. If you are using shrimps, cut them into smaller pieces.

3 Cut the nori sheets into small pieces. In a cup or small bowl, stir the wasabi into the soy sauce. Pour the mixture into four small bowls. Arrange all other ingredients decoratively on a serving platter.

4 To eat the sashimi, hold a slice of fish (or a piece of scallop or shrimp) with your chopsticks, dip it into the spiced soy sauce, and enjoy.

How we celebrate in
JAPAN

People in Japan celebrate many national holidays, plus some that have been introduced from other cultures.

I n Japan, holidays are celebrated to honor the Japanese emperor, to show respect for the elderly and the deceased, and to celebrate nature and the arrival of spring. Children, too, have their own special days.

New Year holiday

Shogatsu is Japan's most important national festival. In the days leading up to New Year, people hold *bonekai* parties to "forget the old year." Then everyone stops work for a three-day holiday. Houses are properly cleaned and decorated with pine, plum, and bamboo twigs. People send postcards to arrive on January 1, and children receive presents.

Families gather to spend time together. They share a meal of soba—long buckwheat noodles that symbolize long life. They watch popular TV shows. As the New Year arrives, the bells ring out in Buddhist temples across the country. They chime 108 times, because Buddhists believe that people have to overcome 108 worldly desires. Many people stay up to watch the sunrise at temples and other beauty spots. On New Year's Day,

people eat *osechi-ryori*. This food consists of neatly prepared delicacies, all beautifully stacked in layers in lacquer boxes. The food is eaten with rice wine and a soup with rice dumplings. No one needs to do much cooking over the New Year holiday.

Bean-throwing ceremony

Setsubun is a traditional spring festival that is held on February 3 or 4. In the past, people burned fish heads to drive away evil spirits. Today, they decorate a holiday tree with a sardine head, a clove of garlic, or an onion. They scatter roasted "happiness beans" in homes and in religious shrines and temples. For good luck, people pick up and eat as many beans as they are years old.

Doll festival

At Hina Matsuri, parents wish their daughters a happy and successful life. This traditional doll festival is held on March 3. Beautifully dressed doll models of the emperor, empress, and their courtiers are displayed on shelves covered with red cloth. The display is often

◁ **Bon Odori** is a traditional summer dance festival enjoyed by people all over Japan. Originally the festivities thanked the Rice Paddock God for a good harvest. People dance to the rhythm of taiko drums.

CHERRY BLOSSOM TIME

The first cherry blossom, or sakura, marks the end of the bone-chilling winter. Every park with sakura trees is packed with people who celebrate together.

decorated with peach blossoms. The dolls can be precious family heirlooms, which are handed down from one generation to another. The dolls often have miniature furniture and other household items, and children offer them tiny rice cakes.

After the festival, each girl needs to put the dolls away quickly. If she doesn't, it is said, she will not get married for a long time.

Golden Week

Golden Week falls between April 29 and May 5 and includes several national holidays. Many Japanese people vacation during that week. April 29 is Showa Day; it was the birthday of Emperor Hirohito, or Showa, who ruled Japan during World War II (1939–1945). The next holiday is Constitution Day. It commemorates May 3, 1947, when Japan's democratic

△ *Traditional dancers* perform in a street. Japanese dances include courtly and religious as well as theatrical dances.

constitution was written. This is followed by Greenery, or Nature, Day on May 4, when people celebrate the beauty of the natural world. The final holiday is Children's Day; it is celebrated on May 5 *(see page 28)*.

Star Festival

Tanabata, or Star Festival, celebrates the tale of two lovers who can only meet once a year, on July 7, when two stars cross paths in the Milky Way. Today people write wishes and poems on strips of colored paper. They tie the papers to trees made from bamboo. Tanabata competitions are held around the country for the best decorations. In the city of Sendai, people make seven different kinds of paper decorations. Children sing a song about rustling bamboo leaves and stars.

Festival of Souls

Bon, or Obon, is a Buddhist festival. It is held in mid-July or August to celebrate the spirits of the ancestors. Bon is a time for decorating family graves. People also clean their homes and light fires to welcome in the spirits of the dead. They pray at their home altars and decorate these with paper lanterns. They also make food offerings. People dance to comfort the dead, and they float candle-lit lanterns to guide the spirits home on water.

△ *A samurai and a geisha figure* are two of the dolls at the Nihonmatsu Chrysanthemum Festival in October. The chrysanthemum is Japan's national flower, and 30,000 chrysanthemums decorate the festival dolls.

FESTIVAL LUNCHBOX

Bento lunchboxes (small lacquer boxes) are popular for eating on the go, at festivals, or while traveling.

let's make...
SOBA NOODLE SOUP

We eat noodle dishes at many festivals. The longer the noodles, the better—they are symbolic of a long life. So we like to serve them to older relatives, and wish them many more years.

▽ Oodles of noodles! In Japan it's quite ok to eat noodles with a lot of slurping…

WHAT YOU NEED:

SERVES 4 PEOPLE:

2 eggs
2 ounces baby leaf spinach or other tender leaf vegetables
1 small carrot
2 green onions
1 sheet nori seaweed
1 lb soba noodles
2½ pints dashi stock *(see page 41)*
light soy sauce for flavoring

WHAT'S THIS: soba?

Real soba noodles are very long and thin, and they're made from buckwheat, a type of cereal. In Japan we call all thin noodles *soba*, even if they're not made from buckwheat. Thick noodles are called *udon*.

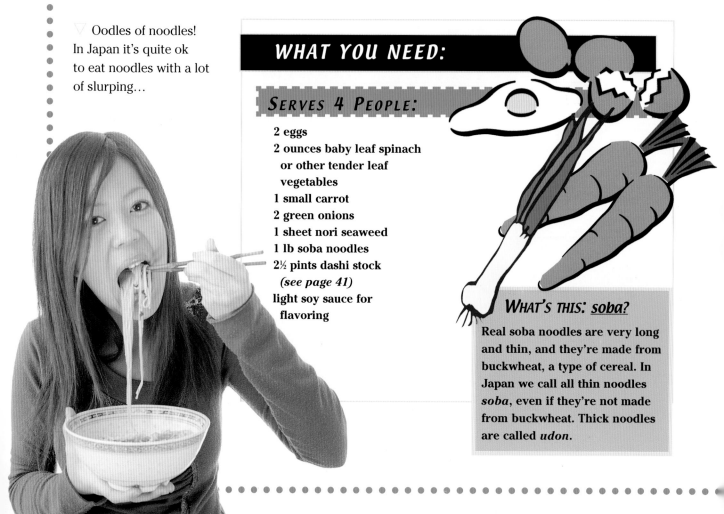

1 Pierce each egg once with a skewer. Put the eggs in a saucepan with boiling water and boil them hard for 8 minutes. Refresh the eggs under cold running water, then peel them. Allow to cool, then slice the eggs.

2 Wash the spinach; throw away wilted leaves. Cut the spinach into strips. Peel the carrot; cut it into very thin slices. Wash and trim the green onions, then cut them into thin slanted rings. Cut the nori into very thin strips.

3 In a large saucepan, bring plenty of water to a boil. Add the noodles and cook for about 5 minutes.

4 In another saucepan, heat the dashi. Add the vegetables and cook for 2 minutes. Add a little soy sauce. Drain the noodles in a sieve and divide them between four soup bowls.

5 Ladle the soup over the noodles. Add the egg and nori strips. Serve and slurp!

let's make...
TAMAGOYAKI

These rolled omelets are popular at all occasions, for festivals and everyday eating, too. They are also delicious cold, so they are ideal for lunchboxes or a quick afternoon snack.

▽ Tamagoyaki are perfect for Japanese-style picnic boxes. We also take along sushi and pickles, especially pickled ginger. Then we go to a park, sit down on a large blanket, and enjoy our Japanese "takeout."

WHAT YOU NEED:

SERVES 4 PEOPLE:

8 eggs
5 tablespoons dashi
   (or chicken broth)
2 teaspoons sugar
4 teaspoons soy sauce
3 tablespoons green parts
   of green onions, finely
   chopped
a little oil for frying

HOW WE COOK THE <u>omelet</u>

In Japan, we use a square frying pan to make tamagoyaki. This makes it easier to shape the omelet into regular long rolls.

MY TIP

These omelet rolls are perfect for *bento*, which is what we call our lunchboxes.

1 Crack the eggs into a bowl and beat them with a fork. Stir in the dashi, sugar, soy sauce, and the green onion pieces.

2 Heat a little oil in a deep omelet skillet over low heat. Keep the heat really low, so the sugar in the mix does not make the omelet burn. !

3 Put one ladle of the egg mixture into the skillet. Turn the skillet from side to side, so the bottom of the skillet gets covered with egg mixture.

4 When the egg has set, carefully roll up the omelet from one side toward the center. Leave it in the skillet.

5 Put some more oil in the skillet, and add more egg mixture. Slip the egg under the finished omelet too. Fry until it is almost but not completely set. !

7 Continue frying more omelets and rolling them around finished ones until all the egg is used up. Take the omelet roll out of the skillet. Place it on a bamboo roll or a clean kitchen cloth and flatten it. Once it has cooled, cut it into 1-inch slices and serve. !

6 Now roll this second omelet around the first one, to make it into a thicker roll.

How we celebrate at home in
JAPAN

A part from the national and regional festivities, there are also many events that families celebrate privately. In Japan, reaching a particular age is an important reason to celebrate.

Seven-Five-Three Festival

In Japan, a child's third, fifth, and seventh birthdays are the most important birthdays in his or her life. On the weekend closest to November 15, the Seven-Five-Three Festival, or Shichi-Go-San, takes place. On this day, parents take their sons between the ages of three and five, and their daughters between the ages of three and seven to a local Shinto shrine. Here they pray that their children will stay healthy and have a long life.

Children wear their best clothes, which may be Japanese or Western in style. Traditional outfits include silk kimonos with sandals or matching slippers for girls, and jackets and *hakama* (folded, skirtlike pants) for boys.

Children's Day

From the end of April until Children's Day, on May 5, colorful carp-shaped windsocks called *koinobori* flutter in the wind all over Japan. Once this holiday was a celebration just for boys, but now girls celebrate too. The koi carp is a symbol of strength. This is

COSTLY KIMONOS

Today, many women only have one kimono. These robes can be as expensive as a new car to buy. So women often just rent a complete outfit, even for their wedding day.

◁ **For the Coming of Age Day**, girls wear special *furisode kimonos* and *zori* slippers. They go out in town and celebrate with their friends who have also become adults that day.

because an ancient Chinese legend tells the story of a carp that swam up a waterfall and turned into a dragon.

Warrior dolls and helmets are on display to symbolize strength. Some homes place the armor and weapons of samurai warrior models in special niches. Boys wear paper helmets and eat sweet rice cakes with their families.

Coming of Age Day

When young people turn twenty in Japan, they officially become adults and have new duties. This is known as *Seijin hi*, or Coming of Age Day. It is a national holiday on the second Monday in January. Everyone celebrates at the same time, even if their birthday is not on that day. The boys wear kimonos or suits, and the girls wear kimonos with white fur collars. They visit Shinto shrines and have their photo taken.

Mother's Day

Mother's Day, or *Haha no hi*, is celebrated on the second Sunday in May. Children give their mother red carnations or other gifts. They help out with chores at home and cook a meal, or go out as a family to a restaurant. At school, many children make special gifts for their mother or draw a picture.

Father's Day falls on the third Sunday in June. Some schools hold special Sunday classes, so that busy fathers can see first-hand how their children are doing at their studies.

The tea ceremony

The traditional Japanese tea ceremony, or *chaji*, has many formal rules. Learning how to prepare and serve tea properly can take years.

The host dresses in formal clothes and prepares and serves the tea in a special tea house, which often stands in the garden. The type of tea used is powdered green leaves called *maccha*. The powder is stirred with a bamboo whisk. The ceremony includes many ritual gestures, both for the host and for the guest, which have to be learned.

Weddings

Weddings usually take place in the spring or the fall. Although many people are not very religious today, the wedding ceremonies are

▽ **Chashitsu** is a room that has been specially designed for the tea ceremony. The host prepares for days for the ceremony. He or she makes sure that everything is perfect when the guests arrive.

quite formal. They follow Buddhist, Shinto, or Christian traditions. The couple say their marriage vows, drink sake, and exchange their glasses. The guests join them for the wedding reception. They bring money gifts for the couple in red envelopes.

Christmas

Aside from Buddhist and Shinto festivals, some people also celebrate Christian holidays such as Christmas Day. They set up Christmas trees in their homes, and parents give their children presents. For some Buddhists, a monk called Hotei-osho comes in place of the Western Santa Claus and brings the presents.

△ **This Japanese snowman** looks like a Christmas tree. Many people also decorate the outside of their homes with Christmas lights.

◁ **Red and white** are lucky colors in Japan. The bride and groom make sure they wear something that is red. The food that is served at the wedding banquet is also red in color.

let's make...
SUKIYAKI

This dish is a bit like a Western fondue. It's prepared directly at the table. For special occasions, people sit all around the table and cook their own food.

▽ A gas burner or a tea warmer with tealight candles is perfect for keeping the skillet hot while we cook our food.

WHAT YOU NEED:

SERVES 4 PEOPLE:

1 lb 2 ounces fillet of beef
4 ounces glass noodles
2 bunches green onions
3 large carrots
12 ounces fresh shiitake mushrooms
9 ounces tofu
⅔ cups soy sauce
⅔ cups vegetable stock
1 tablespoon beef tallow (or cooking oil)
3 teaspoons sugar
white pepper
your favorite dipping sauces

HOW DO I EAT sukiyaki?

Put a slice of meat in the stock and cook it for 5 minutes, then push it to the edge of the skillet. Pour in a little more stock. Add some of the other ingredients and cook for a few minutes. The sauce should only just cover the bottom of the skillet. Everyone now picks out with chopsticks what they'd like to eat and dips the food in their favorite sauce. Continue cooking more meat and vegetables, and adding stock.

1 Wash the meat and pat it dry. Cut it into thin slices. Put the noodles into a bowl, pour boiling water over them, and leave them to soak.

2 Wash and trim the green onions. Cut the white parts into thin, slanted rings. Cut the green parts into 2-inch lengths, and cut these into matchsticks. Peel and chop the onion. Wipe the mushrooms clean with a damp cloth, then cut them into thick strips.

3 Drain the tofu and cut it into cubes. Drain the glass noodles in a sieve. Leave them long! Stir the soy sauce into the stock. Set out all the ingredients. Put the dipping sauces into small bowls.

4 Heat the tallow or cooking oil in a wide skillet on top of the stove. Sprinkle in the sugar and stir until it turns to caramel. Pour in a little of the soy stock—do this very carefully and from a distance! It could splatter and burn you. Keep the sauce hot on the gas burner or tea warmer.

let's make...
TEMPURA

For this festive dish we coat food in a very light batter. The batter is so light that you can see the color of the vegetables underneath. We also cook fish and seafood this way.

▽ I sprinkle my tempura pieces with grated radish and dip them in a sauce of dashi *(see page 41)*, mirin, and shoyu.

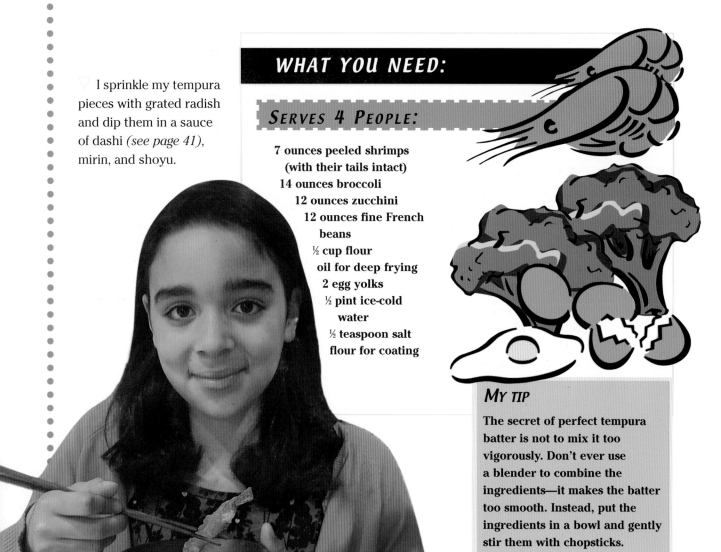

WHAT YOU NEED:

SERVES 4 PEOPLE:

7 ounces peeled shrimps
(with their tails intact)
14 ounces broccoli
12 ounces zucchini
12 ounces fine French
beans
½ cup flour
oil for deep frying
2 egg yolks
½ pint ice-cold
water
½ teaspoon salt
flour for coating

MY TIP

The secret of perfect tempura batter is not to mix it too vigorously. Don't ever use a blender to combine the ingredients—it makes the batter too smooth. Instead, put the ingredients in a bowl and gently stir them with chopsticks.

1 Cut the broccoli into smaller pieces. Slice the zucchini and halve very large slices. Cut the ends off the beans, but leave them whole. Wash the shrimps under cold water, drain them, and pat them dry. Wash and trim the vegetables.

3 Put all the vegetable pieces and shrimps into a plastic bag, add the flour, and close. Shake well to coat everything with flour. Place all the pieces on a large platter.

4 When you are ready to eat, make the batter. Combine the egg yolks, the ice-cold water, the flour, and the salt *(see My Tip on the left)*. Put the batter into individual bowls so each person can cook their own tempura.

2 Bring plenty of water to a boil in a large saucepan. Briefly cook one vegetable at a time—broccoli for 4 minutes, zucchini 2 minutes, beans 5 minutes—all should still be crunchy. Lift out the half-cooked vegetables with a slotted spoon and rinse them under cold water. Drain. In a fondue pot, heat the oil for deep frying. Keep the oil hot over a flame.

5 To cook tempura, hold a shrimp or vegetable with your chopsticks (or with a fork), dip them in the batter, then hold them into the hot fat. Take out after 1 minute. It's ready to eat, but be careful not to burn your mouth—it is very hot!

How we live in
JAPAN

People in Japan live mainly in the large cities, and the most important city is the capital, Tokyo. Aside from their home lives, school and the workplace are very important to people. Once, men were the only breadwinners, while women looked after the home and cared for children and the elderly. This is changing here as elsewhere.

The Japanese home

A traditional Japanese house is made of wood. It is supported by wooden posts. The floors are covered with a woven straw mat, called a *tatami*. People used to sleep on the floor on futons that can be rolled up and put away during the day to make a living room.

Today, most families live in houses or apartment buildings similar to those in the West. But they still have at least one room that is furnished with a tatami mat. Before entering a Japanese home, people take off their shoes and put on slippers.

Today, people only wear a *kimono* on special days. A kimono is a long silk robe that is tied at the waist with a wide belt called an *obi*. Children wear shorter kimonos called *yakuta*. Everyday clothes are casual and international in style.

People entertain friends mostly outside their homes because there is normally very little space for guests.

▽ *These schoolchildren* are asking for good luck in their exams. They buy pieces of paper called *omikuji* at a Shinto temple. As in a lottery, the papers may contain greater or lesser blessings.

ALL ABOARD

At busy times, some subway trains in Tokyo get so crowded that special "people pushers" called oshiya have to help push more people onto the trains before the doors close!

City life

Japan's cities are busy and crowded, but there are plenty of things to do in the cities. People visit beautiful gardens and parks, playgrounds, historic buildings, museums, theme parks, zoos, and aquariums. Travel on the subway is quick and cheap. But the trains get very crowded at the start and the end of the working day. Eleven million people commute to work in Tokyo each day; they come on buses, trains, and subways.

Country life

Fewer than a fourth of all people in Japan live in the countryside. Life there is not as fast-paced as in the large cities and their suburbs. But life can be hard in the countryside too. Work in the fields is backbreaking. Many people from farming villages have to travel a long distance into towns and cities to find work so they can get by.

School classes in Japan's remote mountain and fishing villages often have very few pupils. Children also travel far to their nearest school, either on foot or by bus. But in small villages people know each other. They often stop for a chat and help each other in times of need. So people in villages are rarely lonely, and the elderly are often well cared for.

Life at school

Most children in Japan go to excellent state schools. Children start school the April before they are six years old. They spend three years in elementary school and three in a middle school, then they go on to high school.

The main subjects at school are reading and writing, math, science, social studies, music, crafts, physical education, and home economics. There are 2,000 characters in the Japanese language, so learning to write is difficult. Many children also learn calligraphy. This is the art of writing beautiful letters with a brush and ink. Pupils bring *bento* lunchboxes from home. These include tasty foods, such as sushi or omelets called *tamagoyaki*.

> ▽ **Students learn** to play Western musical instruments such as violins. Today they also learn about Japan's own musical traditions. Playing ancient instruments, such as the *koto* (zither), *shakuhachi* (flute), and *taiko* (drum), is also part of their lessons.

△ **Shinkansen** are fast Japanese trains that connect the major cities. These were the first high-speed trains in the world, and they hold the world speed record of 361 miles per hour.

fishing, and going to the beach. Sumo wrestling is Japan's national sport. People also enjoy going to festivals, visiting museums and parks, and admiring the cherry blossom in spring and leaf colors in fall.

Time off

After a busy day at school, children have many activities to choose from. Some children join sports clubs to play baseball, basketball, martial arts, soccer, tennis, or swimming. At home, they relax with video and computer games, and watch cartoons on TV. Family activities include hiking, cycling, skiing,

Meal times

Traditionally, the family used to sit around a low table on tatami mats. Each person picked up food from the serving dishes with their chopsticks and put them into their own bowl. Today, parents and children spend long hours at work and school. They have less time to prepare fresh food and eat more fast food.

let's make...
MISO SOUP

We eat miso soup almost every day—for breakfast, after school, and before other dishes at dinner. It is delicious and comforting, and it aids digestion.

▽ You can eat the leeks and tofu in this soup with chopsticks. But try eating the soup itself like that!

WHAT YOU NEED:

SERVES 4 PEOPLE:

5–6 ounces Japanese tofu
2 thin leeks
a piece fresh ginger,
    about ¾ inch long
3½ cup dashi stock
4 tablespoons miso
    (soybean paste)

WHAT'S THIS: miso?

Miso is a soybean paste. It is made from fermented soybeans or grains, such as rice. We use miso in many different dishes.

MY TIP

Dashi is the base for many soups and sauces in Japan—so make a larger amount and freeze it.

1 Wash the tofu under cold water and cut it into 1-inch cubes. Wash the leek, cut off all wilted leaves. Cut the leeks into very thin rings or strips and wash it again. **!**

2 Peel the ginger, then grate it finely. Squeeze it with your fingers. Save the juice and throw the ginger away.

3 Heat the dashi stock in a large saucepan, but do not let it boil. Put the miso paste into a bowl. Stir a little stock into the miso. **!**

! ## HOW DO I MAKE _dashi_ STOCK?

To make four portions of dashi, buy a piece of konbu (a dried seaweed) of about 6 by 6 inches. Wipe it with a clean cloth, but do not wash it with water. Cut the konbu into wide strips, and place these in a saucepan.

Add 1¾ pint water and bring it to a boil over medium heat. As soon as the water starts to bubble, take the saucepan off the heat. Lift out the konbu.

Stir the bonito flakes into the water and return to a boil. Take the saucepan off the heat. Leave it for about 1–2 minutes, until the bonito flakes have sunk to the bottom of the pan.

Line a sieve with a fine cloth. Pour the dashi through the sieve. Continue as above, from Step 3.

4 Now add the miso–stock mixture to the rest of the dashi stock, a little at a time. Stir in the tofu, leeks, and ginger juice. Serve hot.

let's make...
CHICKEN & EGG DOMBURI

This is a typical midweek meal. People often eat domburi after a bowl of miso soup, sometimes even for breakfast. It is a rice dish, with a topping of chicken and mushrooms.

▽ If you hold the bowl close to your mouth, you can make sure that none of this delicious food drops off your chopsticks.

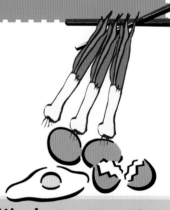

WHAT YOU NEED:

SERVES 4 PEOPLE:

1⅓ cup short-grain
  Japanese rice
salt
1 large boneless chicken
  breast, without skin
1 cup fresh shiitake
  mushrooms
1 bunch tender green
   onions
  1 cup strong chicken stock
  6 tablespoons light
    soy sauce
  6 eggs

WHAT'S THIS: *domburi?*

Domburi is the Japanese word for bowl, because we always eat this dish out of a bowl. The chicken and egg topping is also known as *oyako domburi.* That means "mother and child domburi." Why? Because it contains chicken—and egg!

1 Put the rice into a saucepan with lightly salted boiling water. Cook for about 15 minutes. Drain and cover the pan to keep the rice warm.

2 Wash the chicken under cold water. Pat it dry with paper towels. Cut the chicken into very thin strips.

3 Cut off any wilted parts from the mushrooms. Wipe the mushrooms clean with moist paper towels. Wash and trim the green onions. Cut the onions into very thin slanted rings.

4 Heat the stock in a wok, add the soy sauce, the chicken strips, mushrooms, and green onions. Cook everything for about 3 minutes.

5 Crack the eggs into a small bowl and beat them with a fork. Pour the mixture into the wok. Cook over a gentle heat for 2 minutes, until the egg mix has set (becomes firm).

6 Divide the rice between individual bowls. Spoon the chicken-egg-mixture over the top and serve.

let's make...
GREEN TEA
ICE CREAM

Hokkaido, in northern Japan, has many dairy farms. This delicious and refreshing dessert combines milk and cream with the best Japanese tea, from Shizuoka.

▽ This delicious ice cream is a dessert choice in many Japanese snack bars and restaurants. And now I can make it myself!

WHAT YOU NEED:

SERVES 4 TO 6 PEOPLE:

2 tablespoons maccha green
   tea powder
⅓ cup hot water
2 egg yolks
¾ cup milk
2 tablespoons sugar
¾ cup heavy cream

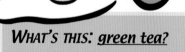

WHAT'S THIS: green tea?

Green tea is the most popular drink in Japan. Tea farms are everywhere, especially in the Shizuoka area. Maccha powder is made by grinding steamed and dried green tea leaves into a powder, using a stone mortar.

1 Put the green tea powder and the hot water into a bowl. Stir well, then set the bowl to one side. **!**

2 Put the egg yolks into a small high saucepan. Beat them with a fork until they are smooth. Stir in the milk and the sugar. **!**

3 Heat the egg and milk mixture over a very low heat. Stir all the time, until the mixture thickens. **!**

4 Put plenty of ice-cold water and ice cubes into a large bowl. Place the saucepan with the egg mixture into this bowl. Stir in the tea powder. In a jug, whisk the cream until it is stiff.

5 Gently stir the stiff cream into the egg and tea mixture, using a figure-eight motion. When all is combined, put the mixture into the freezer for at least 3 hours. Serve cold.

HOW DO I MAKE <u>green tea?</u>

People make and drink different teas at different temperatures in Japan. To make maccha tea, put 1 teaspoon of powder into your tea pot. Add 6 cups hot water at 160°F and stir well with a bamboo tea whisk.

Look it up
JAPAN

bento a Japanese lunchbox with compartments for several different dishes, often including sushi and tamagoyaki

dashi a Japanese broth or stock, the base for miso and other soups and sauces

green tea the typical Japanese tea; it is drunk daily and served during the tea ceremony; it is also an ingredient in many dishes

kimono the traditional silk dress worn by Japanese women; there are many versions

miso a traditional food made from fermented soybeans and other ingredients; miso is a part of miso soup, which is drunk before meals or for breakfast

omikuji a paper fortune that can be bought at a Shinto temple

shinkasen the Japanese high-speed train, known as the bullet train in the West; it was the first high-speed train in the world, and it is the holder of the world speed record

Shinto the main Japanese religion

soba long, thin buckwheat noodles: a symbol of longevity, or a long life

sushi a rolled food made from vinegared rice and vegetables or seafood, often wrapped in nori seaweed

tamagoyaki a Japanese rolled omelet, made from several layers of set egg

torii an entrance gate before a Shinto shrine, sometimes it seems to be floating in water

tofu a beancurd made from soybeans; part of many vegetarian meals in Japan

Find out more
JAPAN

Books to read

Case, Robert.
Countries of the World: Japan.
Facts On File, 2003.

Messager, Alexandre, and Duffet, Sophie.
We Live in Japan (Kids Around the World).
Abrams Books for Young Readers, 2007.

Reynolds, Jeff.
Japan (A to Z).
Children's Press, CT, 2005.

Wiltshire, Diane, and Huey, Jeanne.
Japan for Kids: The Ultimate Guide for Parents and Their Children.
Kodansha International, 2000.

Web sites to check out

www.japan-guide.com
A travel web site with a good A–Z section on the arts, culture, food, history, and more

http://web-japan.org/kidsweb
A children's web site including recipes, culture notes, legends, and "cool stuff"

www.japaneselifestyle.com.au/culture/culture.html
All about Japanese culture, with entries on geishas, festivals, calligraphy, and more

www.japan-guide.com/e/e620.html
All about Japanese food, with information on ingredients and recipes

www3.nationalgeographic.com/places/countries/country_japan.html
The National Geographic magazine's site on Japan

Index

JAPAN